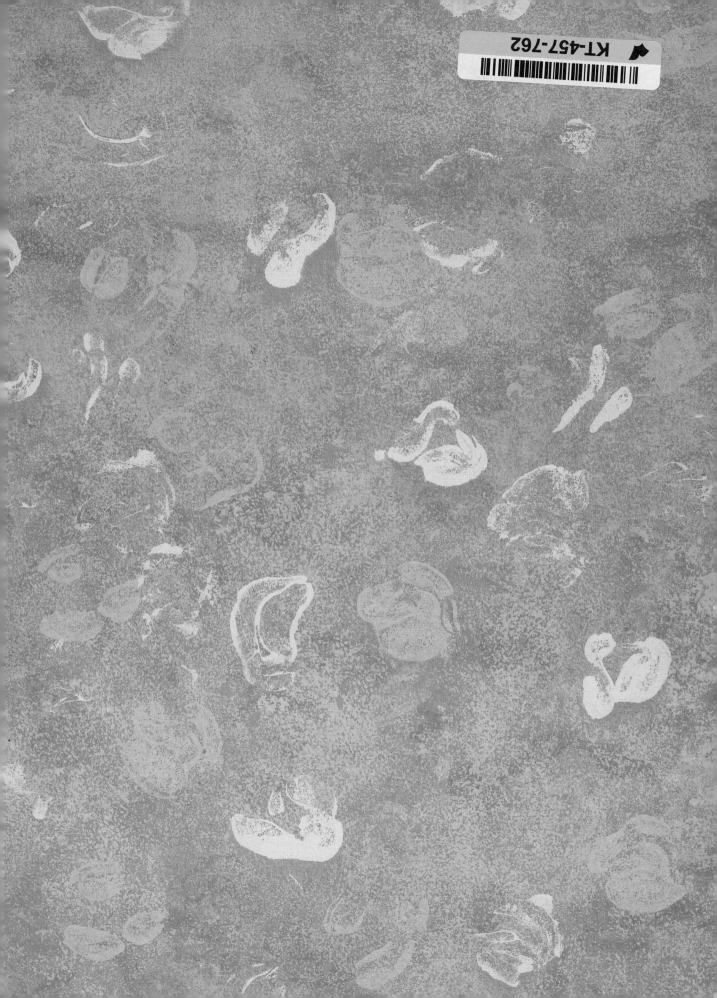

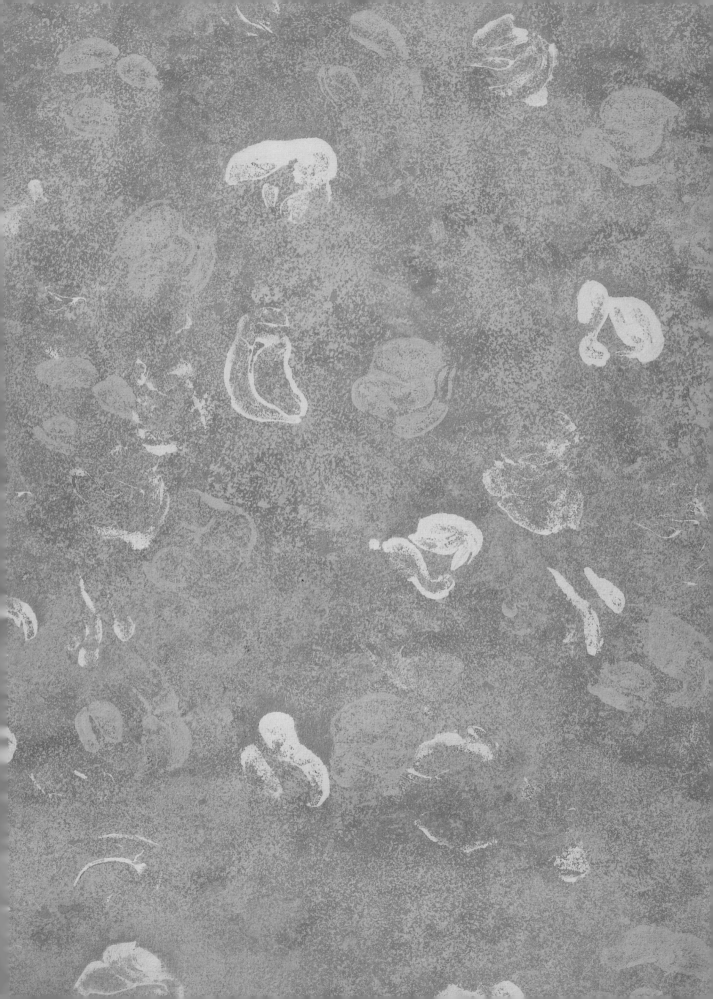

The Adventures of Odysseus

The Adventures

A Dolphin ★ Paperback
from Orion Children's Books

ITALY

Island of Aeolus

The Sirens

Nausicaa

Circe's Enchanted Isle

The Cyclops

SICILY

Scylla & Charybdis

Hyperion's Cattle

The Lotus Eaters

Calypso's Isle

# of Odysseus

Retold by NEIL PHILIP
Illustrated by PETER MALONE

Fall of Troy

GREECE

TURKEY

Ithaca

CRETE

For Michael and Elizabeth Barrott
N.P.

For L.J.M
P.M.

Published in paperback in 1997
First published in Great Britain in 1996
by Orion Children's Books
a division of the Orion Publishing Group Ltd
Orion House
5 Upper St Martin's Lane
London WC2H 9EA

Text copyright © Neil Philip 1996
Illustrations copyright © Peter Malone 1996

A catalogue record for this book is available from the British Library

Designed by Dalia Hartman
Printed in Italy

Contents

ATHENE
Goddess of wisdom and war, Zeus's daughter

ZEUS
Ruler of the gods

POSEIDON
God of the sea, Zeus's brother

AEOLUS
God of the winds

HERMES
Messenger of the gods

HYPERION
The sun god

CIRCE *and* CALYPSO
Goddess of enchantment *Goddess of silence*

POLYPHEMUS
A Cyclops, the son of Poseidon

Mortals

ODYSSEUS
Son of Laertes, King of Ithaca

PENELOPE
Wife of Odysseus

TELEMACHUS
Son of Odysseus

MENELAUS
King of Sparta, husband of Helen

HELEN
Zeus's daughter, Menelaus's wife; her abduction by Paris caused the   war of Troy

AGAMEMNON
Leader of the Greeks in the war with Troy

NAUSICAA
Daughter of King Alcinous

ALCINOUS
King of the Phaeacians

EUMAEUS
a swineherd loyal to Odysseus

The Lotus-Eaters

The city of Troy was in flames.

Odysseus looked back, and laughed.

For ten bitter years the Greek army had laid siege to the city. Now at last they had done what they came to do. The walls of Troy, built by the god Poseidon himself, were tumbled to the ground. Paris, Prince of Troy, who had dared to steal away the beautiful Helen from King Menelaus, was dead. Now they could go home.

It was not much, perhaps, Odysseus's home. Ithaca – a poor, bare, low-lying island far out to the west; the island of the setting sun. But every man loves the land where he is born, and no place on earth was dearer to Odysseus than Ithaca. For all those years that the Greeks had warred against Troy, his heart was yearning for his home.

The soil of Ithaca may be thin and starved, but it grows true sons. Odysseus had left one behind: Telemachus. He thought often of his son and his wife Penelope, and longed to be with them.

In truth, he had never wanted to leave them. What did he care if Paris had taken a fancy to Menelaus's wife Helen? When Agamemnon, Menelaus's brother, who led the Greek army against Troy, came to collect Odysseus to join the expedition, he had pretended to be mad. He yoked a horse and a bull together to plough the seashore, and sow it with salt. But they pushed his son Telemachus into his path. Odysseus swerved to avoid him, and they saw through the act.

"Odysseus, you shall plan for us," said King Agamemnon. "For your cunning may win where strength fails."

Cunning, indeed, was needed, where the strength and bravery of the two sides was so finely balanced. It was Odysseus who came up with the plan to deceive the Trojans into opening their city gates, so letting the

finest Greek soldiers into the city, concealed in a wooden horse. Then Troy was put to the fire and the sword.

Of all the leaders of the Greeks, Odysseus was the most eager to be on his way. He called his men to him, and they set sail, while the sky behind them still burned red.

But bad luck was with them from the start. Great Zeus, who wields the thunder and lightning, sent such storms that their ships bucked and plunged in the waves like frightened horses. The rain scoured all colour from the world, until they could not tell the sea from the sky. The wind tore their sails to shreds. There was nothing they could do but pull for shore.

There they lay, weary and sick at heart, for two days and nights while the storm blew itself out. On the third day, they set sail once more, only to be caught by fierce currents that pulled them far off course. They were dragged south by the relentless wind and waves for ten whole days, until at last they reached land.

They went ashore and soon found fresh water. Odysseus sent a party of men inland, to find out who lived in this hot far-off country.

None of them returned.

At last Odysseus himself went in search of them. In a clearing, he found one of his men. He was lying on his back, humming a tune. Odysseus recognized the melody; it was an old Ithacan lullaby, such as every mother croons to her baby.

The man hardly seemed to recognize Odysseus. Instead he held out some fruit, saying, "Here, have some." His voice was slurred, and juice from the ripe fruit was dribbling down his chin.

Odysseus slapped his cheek to bring him round. Little by little, the story came out. This was the land of the Lotus-Eaters – so-called because their only food was the honeyed lotus fruit. They had offered their fruit to Odysseus's men. Whoever tasted it once, lived only to taste it again.

Odysseus tried to reason with the man. "Don't you want to come home?" he asked.

"I'm already home," the man mumbled, his mouth full of fruit. He began to slip once more into his waking dream, and nothing Odysseus said could stir him from it.

Odysseus returned to the ships and fetched more men, cautioning them not to eat the lotus fruit. One by one, they dragged their blank-eyed, smiling companions back to the ships. They tied them up, and fled from that deadly land, where men are trapped by the lotus fruit in a trance of childhood.

As the oars dipped once more into the whitening sea, they tried to shut their ears to the piteous cries of those men who had eaten the lotus fruit.

In the Cave of the Cyclops

Odysseus and his men sailed on, sad and weary, until they came to the country of the Cyclopes. These huge, fierce beings have only one eye right in the centre of their foreheads. They do no work, relying instead on the goodwill of Zeus, whose thunderbolts they make. So, although they neither plough nor sow, still their crops grow. They live in caves high in the hills, and each of them makes his own laws.

The crews beached the boats in a fine harbour, close to a spring of fresh water and a grove of black poplars. They slaughtered some goats, and ate and drank, then slept at ease in this delightful spot.

When the first flush of dawn was in the sky, Odysseus picked twelve of his men and set out to explore. They climbed until they came to a cave, with a courtyard of wood and stone. It was clearly the home of some

14

shepherd, for there were sheep and goats in pens, and also many huge cheeses in baskets.

"Let us take as many of these cheeses as we can carry, drive the animals on to the boats, and set sail before this shepherd returns," said Polites, one of Odysseus's most trusted companions. "From the looks of it, he must be a giant."

But Odysseus replied, "No, let us wait, and greet him when he returns from his pastures. He may be master of all this land, and if he knows what is due from host to guest, will give us gifts."

So they made themselves at home in the Cyclops's cave. They lit a fire and killed a sheep. After they had offered the gods the portion due to them, they ate. At last they heard the heavy tread of the Cyclops, whose name was Polyphemus. From a distance, he looked more like some vast mountain crag than flesh and blood. Their courage failed, and they hid in a dark corner of the cave, meaning to creep out when they could.

But when Polyphemus came home, driving his flocks and carrying a huge bundle of wood to make a fire, he closed the entrance behind him with an enormous boulder, so big that you couldn't shift it with twenty four-wheeled wagons. Then he settled down to milk the sheep and goats.

Something troubled the Cyclops at his work: a strange scent. He began to sniff the air. Searching the cave, he soon discovered Odysseus and his men, cowering in the corner.

"Who are you, and where do you come from?" he roared.

"We are Greeks, come from the sack of Troy," said Odysseus. "Show us, we beg, the hospitality due to wayfaring guests, as you respect the gods. For Zeus himself looks after travellers."

"And I look after myself," replied Polyphemus. "We Cyclopes do not fear the gods, for we are as strong as they are. Nevertheless I may choose to spare you. Tell me, how did you come here? Did my father Poseidon allow you to travel freely over the waves? Is your ship moored nearby?"

Odysseus, guessing that the giant would destroy their ships and murder the crews, replied, "Our ship was dashed against the rocks by great Poseidon and sank. My companions and I are the only survivors."

Polyphemus asked no further questions. Instead he reached down and plucked two men from the huddled group. He swung them by the ankles and dashed their brains out against the cave wall. Then he tore them limb from limb and devoured them raw, like a ravening animal. The others looked on in terror and dismay. Polyphemus washed his meal down with milk, and lay down to sleep.

As the Cyclops lay snoring on the floor, Elpenor, the youngest of Odysseus's men, urged Odysseus to kill him. "Slide your sword in between his ribs, just there! That should finish him off."

"It would finish us off too", replied Odysseus, "for how could we escape? Only the Cyclops is strong enough to budge the rock that seals us in here. No, we must wait and see what the new day brings."

At dawn, Polyphemus rose, and made a gruesome breakfast from two more of Odysseus's companions. He gathered his flocks and set out for the pastures, closing the rock door behind him. Odysseus and the remaining eight men were left to tremble in the cave, waiting for nightfall and the return of the Cyclops.

At last Odysseus spoke. "It may be that this Cyclops will eat us all, and that our only choice is between a swift or a slow death. But it may be that we can fool this giant. I have with me a goatskin full of dark red wine, given me by the priest of Apollo. This wine is so potent that it should be diluted with twenty parts of spring water. I shall offer it to the Cyclops tonight, and if he drinks he will fall into a fuddled sleep. Then we must make our move."

Polyphemus had left a great cudgel of olivewood lying in the cave, so big it could have served as the mast of a ship. Odysseus cut off a length of this, and sharpened the end with his sword. Then he and his men laid it in the ashes of the fire to harden, and finally they hid it out of sight.

Polyphemus returned, and again drove his flocks into the cave, closing the entrance behind him.

The Cyclops gorged himself once more on human flesh, and then sat down to drink some milk. Odysseus went up to him, saying, "Cyclops! You have caused my companions to drink the black wine of death. If you are to feast on men's flesh, you should at least send them on their way with honour. I have here a goatskin of fine wine, which I had brought to you as a gift. Let me pour you a bowlful."

The Cyclops drained the bowl in a single swig. Wiping his great blubbery lips, he said, "Tell me your name, little man, for I wish to make you a present in return for this wine. And pour me some more."

Three times Odysseus filled the bowl; three times the Cyclops drank it down. At last, the fumes from the wine began to fog his head. And then Odysseus said, "You ask my name, and I will tell you. It is Nobody."

"Well, Nobody, I will eat you last. That is my gift to you," replied Polyphemus. As the wine overcame him, he sank to the floor. His great head lolled to one side, and as sleep tugged him under, he belched forth a vile mouthful of wine and human flesh.

Odysseus and his men took the stake that they had made out of olivewood, and laid it in the fire until it was red hot. Begging courage of the gods, four of the men took the stake and plunged it into the giant's single eye. Odysseus, above, twisted it to and fro to drill it home. The eye bubbled and hissed with a sound like a smith tempering iron in cold water.

Polyphemus awoke shrieking in agony. He plucked the stake from his forehead, and hit out wildly, but Odysseus and his men could easily dodge the blind, blundering giant.

Polyphemus's screams resounded through the hills, waking the other Cyclopes in their high caves. They all rushed to help him. When they arrived outside his cave, they called, "What is the matter? Who is attacking you?"

And Polyphemus replied. "Nobody is attacking me. Nobody has tried to kill me."

The other Cyclopes were puzzled by this answer. But every time they asked Polyphemus who was to blame, he just wailed, "Nobody!"

"If nobody is attacking you, there is nothing we can do. You must ask your father Poseidon for help, if you are suffering some torment of the gods." And the Cyclopes went away.

Polyphemus groped around the cave for Odysseus and his men, but he could not catch them. So he pushed the boulder away from the entrance, and sat there himself, with his great hands outstretched to catch anyone trying to escape.

When dawn came, the sheep began to file out of the cave, as they were accustomed to do, and Polyphemus felt each one as it passed. But crafty Odysseus had tied them together in groups of three, so that a man could cling beneath the belly of the middle one and go undetected. And so his six remaining companions escaped from the cave.

When it was Odysseus's turn, there was only one ram left – a big, fat creature that was the best in all the flock. Odysseus clutched the shaggy fleece tightly and, with his face pressed to its rank-smelling belly, sent it walking towards the giant.

As it passed, Polyphemus hugged it close to him. "It's you, my beauty," he said. "Normally you are the proudest of all, and the first to leave the cave. Today you have lingered, out of sadness for your master. But I promise you, Nobody shall never escape me. Now, join your fellows in the meadow." And he let the ram go.

Once clear of the cave, Odysseus and his men drove the sheep down to the ships, and made haste to put out to sea, knowing that the Cyclopes made no boats and could not follow them on to the salt waves.

When they were the length of a man's shout from the shore, Odysseus cried, "Cyclops! Are you listening? It is I, Nobody! You scoffed at Zeus, and at the hospitality due to a guest. Now you must suffer for your evil ways."

At this the giant was so outraged that he hurled the massive boulder from the cave entrance at the ship. It landed in the sea with such a tremendous crash that the waves from it drove the ship back on to the shore.

As they rowed frantically out to sea again, Elpenor pleaded with Odysseus not to anger the Cyclops further. "Next time," he said, "he may aim better." But Odysseus was too proud to remain silent.

"Cyclops!" he shouted. "If anyone asks who blinded you, tell them it was Odysseus, Prince of Ithaca. It was my wits that breached the walls of Troy, though they were built by Poseidon himself, and it was I who made a fool of you."

Polyphemus let out a terrible groan. "It is my fate that this has happened. A wise man foretold I would lose my sight at the hands of Odysseus. But I thought Odysseus would be a great hero, strong and tall, not a puny weakling like you." Then he stretched out his arms towards the sea, calling, "Great Poseidon, Earthshaker, Lord of the Waves, hear me! If I am your son, and if you are my father, grant me this. May Odysseus never see his home again, or, if he does, let him come alone and friendless to a house of trouble and sorrow."

That was his prayer, and Poseidon heard it.

Then Polyphemus threw another great rock. This one fell just short of the ship, and its waves sent Odysseus and his men out to sea, to join the rest of the ships. There, Odysseus sacrificed the ram on which he had escaped, and prayed to Zeus for his help. But Zeus would do nothing to turn aside the anger of his brother Poseidon.

Goddess of Enchantment

Next Odysseus and his ships came to the island home of Aeolus, who is the warden of the winds. His island floats on the surface of the sea, and all around it is a wall of bronze. Aeolus lives there with his wife and twelve children: six sons and six daughters, who are married to one another. They spend all their time feasting.

For a whole month Aeolus entertained Odysseus and his men, and questioned them closely about the fall of Troy. At last, Odysseus asked Aeolus for his help on the journey home. "Without it, we will never see Ithaca again, for the gods are against us."

Aeolus gave Odysseus an ox-hide bag tied with a silver cord. In it were all the winds, to be let out as they were needed, except for the west wind, which Aeolus commanded to give Odysseus safe passage home.

At first, all went well. After nine days and nine nights, the shore of Ithaca came into sight. Odysseus, who had been keeping lookout all this time, fell asleep, sure that his long journey was nearly over. His crew began to mutter and whisper among themselves.

"He's coming home rich enough," said one.

"Aye," said another. "He has a shipful of spoils from Troy, while we have nothing."

"And now he has this bag full of gold and silver from Aeolus," said another.

"Let's open it," said the first.

And so the foolish, greedy men undid the silver cord around the ox-hide bag, and let out the winds.

At once a fierce tempest arose, buffeting the ships with merciless fury.

One by one, they foundered. They sank to the bottom of the sea, and the waves closed over them.

Soon only Odysseus's ship was left. The warring winds blew it all the way back to Aeolus's island.

He greeted Odysseus with amazement. "What are you doing back here?" he asked. "Did I not give you command of the winds to see you safely home?"

"You did," answered Odysseus, "but my companions betrayed me. They opened the ox-hide bag, and let loose the tempest. I beg you, gather the winds together again, so that I can go home."

"The gods are truly against you," said Aeolus, "and I cannot help you again. Go!"

Odysseus, heavy at heart, turned once more to the open sea. No friendly wind filled his sails this time; instead, the men had to pull on the oars against both wind and wave. And all the time they knew, no matter what course they steered, that Poseidon was waiting for them.

Odysseus and his men eventually made landfall off the island of Aeaea, the home of Circe, goddess of enchantment.

When they had beached the ship, Odysseus climbed a nearby hill to see what could be seen. As he stood gazing over the island, a stag crossed his path, on its way to drink from the river. Odysseus flung his spear and killed it.

"Men," he cried, "our luck is with us once again. Come, let us feast, and tomorrow we shall explore the island."

Next day, Odysseus divided his crew into two parties. He commanded the first, and his cousin Eurylochus, the second. They drew lots as to who should go first, and Eurylochus won. So he and twenty-two men set off inland.

Before long they came to Circe's palace. It stood in a clearing in the woodland and was built of stone. Wild creatures such as lions and wolves roamed outside it, but Circe's power was so great that they did not attack the men, but fawned on them like dogs.

When the party came to the doors of the palace they could hear Circe inside, singing in a lovely lilting voice as she worked at her loom, weaving such dazzling gossamer cloth as goddesses make.

Then Polites said, "There is a woman in the house, singing as she weaves. The whole building rings with the echoes of her voice. Come, let us go in." They entered, with no suspicion in their hearts. Only Eurylochus waited outside, ill at ease.

The goddess welcomed them. She served them wine and sweetmeats, mixing in them drugs that made them forget their country and their loved ones, and long only to serve Circe the goddess of enchantment. Then she touched each of them lightly with her rod, and as she did they turned into bristly, snuffling swine. Their minds remained the minds of men, but when they tried to cry for help, only a grunt came out.

Eurylochus saw it all, and ran back to the ship with the terrible news. The men wanted to sail at once, abandoning Polites and the others but Odysseus would not leave them.

As he made his way to Circe's palace, Odysseus met Hermes the messenger god, with his golden wand and gold-winged sandals. He looked like a boy on the edge of manhood, with the first soft down still on his upper lip. Nevertheless, Odysseus bowed low, knowing he was in the presence of a god.

"Unlucky man," said Hermes. "You can never free your companions from Circe's power. But wait! Here grows a herb that will keep you safe from her witch's potions. It is called *moly*, and while you carry it no harm can come to you.

"Circe will try to drug you. When she touches you with her rod, you must draw your sword as if to strike her. Then she will beg you to be her lover, and you must agree, for she is a goddess. But first make her swear to do you no harm; otherwise, she may steal away your courage and manhood as you lie naked in her bed."

Hermes departed, and Odysseus carried on his way to Circe's palace. When he reached the door he cried out to be let in. Circe welcomed him, ushered him to a chair, and handed him a golden goblet in which she had mixed her magic potion.

When he had drunk, she touched him with her rod, saying, "Now, be off to the pigsty and lie down with your friends." But he remained a man.

He drew his sword and raised it high as if to strike her dead. Circe fell to her knees, and spoke in pleading tones. "Who are you? How is it you can resist my magic? Only one man could have so strong a heart: Odysseus. If you are he, sheathe your sword, and come with me to my bed. There, we may learn to trust one another."

Odysseus answered. "How can I trust you, when you have turned my men into swine? Promise to free them, and to do me no further harm, and I will lie with you willingly."

The goddess gave her promise. She opened the door of the sty, and Polites and the others came trotting out, looking just like full-grown swine. Circe smeared an ointment on them, and their bristles fell away, their snouts receded, and their limbs lengthened. Soon they were standing upright once again, looking younger and more handsome than before.

Then, as Circe's handmaidens prepared her bedchamber, Odysseus went back to the ship, to tell Eurylochus and the others the news. The men would not believe him, and wanted to put straight to sea, but Odysseus told them, "I have given my word to a goddess, and I cannot break it."

When they reached the palace, Circe welcomed them. "Put aside your cares," she said. "Eat, drink, and be merry." For a year, Odysseus's men feasted, while Odysseus kept loving company with the goddess, who bore him a son, Telegonus.

At last, however, they grew homesick, and Odysseus begged Circe to help them to go back to Ithaca.

"You have offended the most powerful of the gods," said Circe, "and I cannot help you. If you want to return to your home, you must ask advice from the wisest of all, the blind seer Teiresias."

"But Teiresias is dead," said Odysseus.

"Yes, you must venture into Hades itself to speak with him. It will be worth the journey, for while the rest of the dead are mere flitting shadows, Teiresias keeps his wits about him still. He alone can tell you what your future holds."

"Who will pilot me on such a voyage?" asked Odysseus. "No sailor has ever undertaken the dark journey to the house of death."

"Do not worry," she replied. "Just hoist your white sail, and the north wind will carry you where you wish to go. Once you have passed the River of Ocean, you will come to the coast of Hades, with its black and blighted trees. There you must leave your ship, and walk into the land of death. When you come to a rock where two rivers meet, dig a trench, and fill it with milk and honey. Add sweet wine, then water, and sprinkle barley-meal upon it. Then, with heartfelt prayers, you must promise that on your return to Ithaca you will make sacrifices to the dead, and to Teiresias especially.

"You must take a ram and a ewe, and sacrifice them. The numberless hordes of the dead will swarm at the scent of blood, but you must hold them back with your sword, until Teiresias arrives. He will answer all your questions."

Odysseus gathered his men, and returned to the ship. But one did not come with them. Young Elpenor, having drunk too much wine, was lying asleep on the palace roof. Hearing his companions calling for him, he leapt up, lost his footing, plummeted to the ground, and broke his neck.

Odysseus meanwhile spoke to his men. "No doubt you think we are heading for home. But we are not. Our destination is Hades where the goddess has told me to seek the advice of the seer Teiresias."

And the men took to sea once more.

The Voyage to Hades

Odysseus and his crew did not have to touch the oars as their ship carried them to the dread land of death. Circe's breeze filled the sail to speed them across the darkening sea to the very spot she had described.

There, Odysseus poured out milk and honey, sweet wine, and water for the dead, and promised them a sacrifice when he should return to Ithaca. With many prayers and invocations, he slaughtered the ram and the ewe, and dark blood filled the trench.

Ghosts flocked to the place of sacrifice, drawn by the vital energy still pulsing from the hot blood. Old men, young girls, battle heroes, peasants – their shades clamoured and jostled about the trench.

At the head of the throng was the ghost of Elpenor.

Odysseus wept to see him in the land of gloom. "We sailed with all speed," he said, "but you have outstripped us."

However, Odysseus would not let any of the shades feast on the blood, until blind Teiresias came, leaning on his golden staff.

"Draw back and let me drink." said Teiresias, "Then I will reveal your future to you."

Odysseus put up his sword, and Teiresias bent to the steaming blood. Then he spoke.

"Prince Odysseus, you have come from the sunlight into the land of shadow, in order to learn your fate. So listen.

"You seek a safe passage home, but this will not be easy. For you have offended the Earthshaker, Poseidon. First, your cunning brought down the walls of Troy, that Poseidon himself had set up. Second, you have blinded his son, the Cyclops Polyphemus.

"You cannot hope to escape the anger of the gods completely. But if you are careful, you and your companions may yet come safely home.

"Be warned, if you arouse the wrath of the gods once more, the reward will be death and misery. If you return home at all it will be late, and alone. You must hope it is not too late. For even now, suitors from many lands are arriving at your palace, and wooing your wife Penelope with fine gifts and finer words. Your son Telemachus is still a boy. How can he protect her?"

Odysseus answered, "I will heed your words. Whatever may befall, I shall not give up hope. When he was still a child, my son Telemachus fell from a fisherman's boat into the salt sea, yet he was not lost. A dolphin carried him on its back safe to shore; that is why the seal on my ring shows a leaping dolphin. In the same way, surely the gods that weave my fate will bring me safely home at last."

After that, Odysseus let each of the shades, one by one, feed on his sacrifice. And as they did so, they seemed to take on substance, and remember themselves again.

Odysseus was stricken to see his mother, Anticleia, among them. "Mother!" he cried. "Tell me, what brought you to this dim land?"

"It was longing for you, my son," she replied.

Odysseus reached across the trench to comfort her. Three times he tried to clasp her, but it was like embracing mist.

Then came the ghost of Agamemnon, who had led the army against Troy. Odysseus asked him, "Did you, too, arouse the anger of Poseidon on your journey home?"

"No." replied Agamemnon. "I sailed home safely, longing for my wife, Clytemnestra. But she and her lover cut me down with an axe as I came from my bath. May the gods save you from such a homecoming, friend."

Odysseus questioned all who came, and they told him their stories. Some still hugged their envies and spites to them like precious treasures. Some remembered golden days and tender words. But none had thought for the future, except the blind seer Teiresias.

The Song of the Sirens

From Hades, Odysseus returned to Aeaea, to thank Circe, and to bury the body of Elpenor, as his ghost had requested.

"Welcome, brave men," she greeted them. "You have faced death undaunted. For most, it is enough to meet death once in a lifetime, but you are fated to do so twice. But now, forget murky Hades. Eat and drink, and in the morning you shall set sail."

Odysseus and his men were glad to be back in the world of light and laughter, and spent that evening celebrating. Next day, Circe bade them farewell, with some last words of advice for Odysseus.

"You must sail past the island of the Sirens. They bewitch passing sailors with their beautiful singing; if you sail too close to them, you will fall under their spell, and that will be the end of you. For though they seem from the sea like lovely maidens, once they have lured you ashore they will turn into hag-like birds of prey. Their island is littered with the bones of men they have trapped and devoured.

"Once safely past the Sirens, more dangers await you. You must choose between two terrible routes. The first is overshadowed by great rocks, known as the Wanderers, because they do not stay still, but clash together, and seem to take pleasure in smashing ships into pieces. Only Jason and the Argonauts have ever passed that way in safety, and that was with the help of the goddess Hera.

"The other route is bounded on one side by cliffs so high that you cannot see the sky above them. Halfway up these cliffs is a dingy cave, in which the monster Scylla lives. Her cry will not frighten you; it is no more worrying than a puppy's yelp. But if you see her you will not forget her. She has twelve dangling feet, and six long necks, each topped with a grisly head, each with three rows of evil teeth. From her cave she fishes in the roaring sea below, scooping out dolphins and sharks and other sea-beasts. She feasts greedily with all her heads from the deck of any passing ship, glutting herself on death.

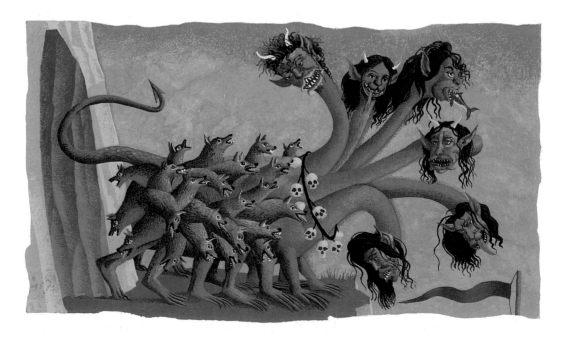

"On the other side, the cliff is lower. A fig-tree grows upon it, but do not steer beneath its shady boughs. For there Charybdis lurks. Three times a day she sucks the dark waters down, then jets them back in a hideous fountain. If you are caught by her, there is no hope for you. Better to steer by Scylla, and lose six men, than for all to perish in the maw of Charybdis."

"Could we not slay these monsters?" asked Odysseus.

"Don't be a fool," replied Circe. "These are deathless creatures, beyond your strength and understanding."

Odysseus set sail once again, worrying about how best to deal with the perils ahead.

As they neared the island of the Sirens, he told his men of the dangers facing them. "We must not listen to the Sirens' song," he said, "or we shall be lost. You must block your ears with soft wax, so that you cannot hear." But Odysseus himself could not pass by the fabled island without hearing the song that was so beautiful it could lure men to their deaths. Again heeding Circe's words, he told his men to lash him to the mast, and made them promise not to release him, even if he commanded them to.

When they drew near to the island, the wind dropped. All was calm and hushed. And into that hush dripped the honeyed notes of the Sirens' song – a song of longing and welcome, of promise and delight. To listen to it was both a rapture and a torment. Odysseus begged and pleaded with his crew to set him free, so that he could follow the song to its source, but they would not, and only bound him tighter to the mast.

Once past the Sirens' isle, Odysseus chose to take the route between Scylla and Charybdis, knowing that no friendly god would speed his ship past the dreadful Wanderers. Soon he could see ahead the crash and spray of the waters. It was a frightening sight, and the roaring of the sea beneath Scylla's cave, together with the low belching sound as Charybdis sucked down the waters and spewed them out again, drained the courage from the rowers, who let their oars dip into the water.

Odysseus urged them, "Be brave! This is no worse than when we were

in the Cyclops's cave. Row! Row for your lives!"

Where Charybdis gulped and vomited the salt waters, the sea swirled in a deadly whirlpool, which would drag any ship to the bottom. There was no choice but to hug the cliff.

Suddenly, from above, Scylla's six fearsome heads swung down, and she seized six of the strongest and best of the crew in her jaws. Odysseus could do nothing as the monster lifted the men screaming into the air, calling his name with heart-rending cries.

As they sailed past, Odysseus and the remaining crew could hear, above the turmoil of the sea, a terrible lapping and crunching as Scylla savoured her grisly meal.

Council of the Gods

After the terrible scene when the monster Scylla devoured six of his men, Odysseus was thankful to arrive at the island of Sicily, where he anchored in a beautiful curving bay.

Now, on that island were the herds of the sun god, Hyperion: seven herds of cows and seven flocks of sheep. Each herd and flock numbered exactly fifty animals; none ever died, and none were born.

"We must leave these animals alone," said Odysseus, "for if we meddle with them, trouble will surely follow." And his men agreed.

But a strong south wind kept them cooped up on the island for a whole month, at the end of which their supplies were exhausted. Odysseus fretted and worried; he begged great Zeus to guide him, and the god granted him that deep sleep which brings new strength and new ideas.

While Odysseus slept, his men lay awake, with hunger gnawing at their stomachs. At last Eurylochus said, "Starvation is the worst of all deaths. Let us feast on the sun god's cattle. When we get back to Ithaca, we can offer sacrifice to Hyperion, and earn his forgiveness." So the men herded up the sun god's cattle, with their long curly horns, and slaughtered them.

When Odysseus awoke and smelt the roasting meat, his heart almost failed. For he knew, as Teiresias had foretold, that a fearful end awaited those who had offended the sun god.

Indeed at that moment Hyperion was standing before Zeus, demanding justice. "Odysseus's crew have slaughtered my cattle, which were my joy. Every day, as I took my path across the sky, I looked down on them with pride and pleasure. Now they are gone. Unless these men pay with their lives, I will go and live in Hades, and shine among the dead."

So when the wind calmed, and the men were able once more to hoist the white sail and take to the sea, their fate was already sealed. Zeus raised a black, violent storm, and blasted the ship with searing thunderbolts.

The ship shivered to pieces, and Eurylochus and all the others were drowned. Only Odysseus survived, clinging to the wreckage. For nine days he drifted helpless on the salt sea, until at last he came to the island of Ogygia, home of Calypso, a goddess with many strange powers.

Calypso, like Circe, fell in love with Odysseus, who had travelled so far across the world, and proved his courage and ingenuity so many times.

"You deserve to be a god," she said. "Marry me, and I will make you immortal."

But Odysseus would not marry her, for he knew in his heart he must return to Penelope and Telemachus.

Yet how could he? He had no ship, and no crew to man one; and besides, Calypso so hedged him about with spells that he could not leave the island. Odysseus spent seven long lonely years sitting on the cliff tops, staring out to sea, and weeping at his fate.

All this time Poseidon, the Earthshaker, kept Odysseus in the glare of his terrible anger.

In Ithaca, Penelope grieved for her absent husband. Suitors from many lands came to Odysseus's palace, hoping to win her hand. "Odysseus is surely dead," they would say, as they lounged at his table, eating his food and drinking his wine. Then they would call for music and dancing, and revel into the night.

Odysseus's son Telemachus was now a young man, handsome and strong. But there was little he could do against the arrogance of the suitors. As for Penelope, she could only fight for time. "I will make my choice among you," she told them, "when I have finished this tapestry, showing my husband Odysseus's great feats against the Trojans. This much I owe to his memory." Each day she worked hard at the tapestry; but each night, while the drunken suitors caroused and sang, she unpicked the work she had done, so the tapestry was never finished.

Now it happened that Poseidon was absent from Mount Olympus, having gone to Ethiopia to receive a great sacrifice of bulls and rams. As the other gods gathered together in the palace of Zeus, Athene, wisest of them all, spoke.

"Often, it is true, these foolish mortals bring their troubles on themselves, while blaming the gods for all their misfortunes. But my heart is wrung for Odysseus, who has been kept so long from his home and family. Even now he is the prisoner of Calypso, the daughter of Atlas, who knows the depths of the sea, and supports the great pillars that keep the earth and the sky apart. Tell me, Zeus, why do you not take pity on him?"

"It is not I, but Poseidon, who cannot forgive Odysseus for blinding his son Polyphemus."

"Then, as Poseidon is not here, let us see if we can help this unfortunate man. Let us send bright Hermes, our messenger, to instruct Calypso to let Odysseus go. I shall go to Ithaca, to rouse the spirit of young Telemachus, Odysseus's son, who has had to endure so many insults from his mother's suitors."

With that, Athene strapped on her sandals of gleaming gold, which carried her like the wind over land or water, and sped down to Ithaca, where she took the form of Mentes, an old friend of Odysseus.

When she arrived at Odysseus's palace, she found the suitors roistering in the courtyard, playing at draughts, swilling wine, and making jokes at the expense of Telemachus. He was pale and tense, but when he saw Mentes he rose, and courteously beckoned him to sit down.

"What news of your father, noble Odysseus?" asked the guest.

"No news," answered Telemachus. "His bones are bleaching in the sun on some far island, or rotting at the bottom of the sea. Do you think if these louts thought there was any chance of his return they would be lolling here? No, they would be running to their ships as fast as their legs could carry them."

"If so great a man as Odysseus had died, the world would know of it. Tell these suitors they are not welcome here, and if they choose to stay, they must suffer the consequences. Then take ship with me, and we will sail in search of news."

Telemachus did as Mentes advised, and they sailed next day for Sparta, to ask King Menelaus for news of Odysseus. And all the time Athene, in the guise of Mentes, was at the side of young Telemachus, shaping the boy into a man, and strengthening his resolve to find his father and defy the suitors.

Cast Ashore

Meanwhile, Zeus sent his messenger Hermes to Calypso's isle.

Hermes sped across the waves, with his golden wand that brings sweet sleep or dispels it, and his golden sandals that carried him, like Athene, swiftly through the air. He dipped and soared above the waves exulting in their salty spray.

He found Calypso in her cave, singing softly and weaving at her loom with a golden shuttle. On the hearth a fire blazed, and the gentle winds wafted the scent of burning cedar and juniper across the island. By the entrance to the cavern was a grove of alders, aspens, and fragrant cypresses, full of owls and falcons and sea-faring birds, while shading the entrance itself was a vine heavy with grapes. Flowery meadows led down to the deep blue sea. Even the god's heart lifted at such beauty.

Calypso welcomed him and offered him nectar, asking, "What brings you here?"

"I am commanded by all-powerful Zeus, to tell you to release luckless Odysseus. It is not his destiny to remain with you. He must build himself a raft to take him to the land of the Phaeacians; they will furnish him with a ship back to Ithaca, his home."

"O cruel Zeus," cried Calypso. "I rescued this man from the sea, when Zeus had shattered his ship with a thunderbolt. I offered him immortality, to live with me and love me in this enchanted place. And now I must let him go. Who will I find then to be my companion?"

Nevertheless, Calypso had to obey the command of Zeus. She went in search of Odysseus, and found him as usual sitting by the shore, gazing out across the sea to where Ithaca lay.

"The deathless gods have taken pity on you, Odysseus," she said. "I am to let you go. So if you wish, you may cut down trees and I will give you tools to make a raft to carry yourself across the sea. I will provide you with food and water and wine. But think, I beg you, of the sorrows and hardships that must lie ahead. You have a choice. Only forget your family, and you can live here with me, in eternal bliss."

"You have a heart to pity me," said Odysseus, "but I have not one to love you. My love is already pledged. I will endure any hardship if I can return to Ithaca."

Odysseus started work at once building his raft. He felled twenty trees, and shaped them with a bronze axe. He pinned the timbers together to make a raft, and built a half deck on it. Then he raised a mast, and fitted a steering oar, and fenced the sides with plaited willows backed with brushwood.

After four days, the raft was ready. So at dawn next day, Calypso bade him farewell. She gave him provisions for his journey and a fair wind to help him on his way, and she watched him far, far into the distance. Now and then the breeze brought to her some lively snatch of a sailor's song that

Odysseus was singing in his high spirits, and she buried even these sad fragments deep in her heart, to treasure through the lonely years to come.

But Calypso was not the only god to hear Odysseus singing. Earthshaker Poseidon, who spans the earth, also heard that merry voice, as he returned from Ethiopia.

"Who has dared to do this?" he bellowed. "This man has not yet paid for his crimes against me!" And Poseidon summoned a raging tempest to stir up the waves.

Odysseus clung to his raft, while it was flung hither and thither by the squalling winds and deep-rolling seas.

But there was one to take pity on him. Ino, who was once a mortal woman but now lives in the sea, rose from the waves like a gull, and settled on the raft. "Poor man," she said, "Poseidon's anger will destroy you if you try to fight him. You must strip off your clothes and trust yourself to the sea, leaving this unlucky craft to its fate. Here, take this scarf. You can swim from here to the land of the Phaeacians, and the scarf will keep you safe from drowning. But once you reach the shore, cast it into the sea so that it will return to me."

Odysseus grasped the scarf, and flung himself into the waves, with only a single plank to cling to.

For two days and nights Odysseus rode the waves, until, exhausted and near the end of his strength, he reached the rocky shore of the land of the Phaeacians. The rocks tore the skin from his hands as he clutched at them. With his last strength he flung Ino's precious scarf back into the sea; then a wave caught him and threw him on to the beach. He lay there like a broken man, with salty brine pouring from his mouth and nostrils.

As Odysseus lay bruised and battered on the Phaeacian shore, Athene sealed his eyes with sleep.

Then the goddess went to the palace of King Alcinous, and to the bedside of his daughter, Nausicaa, a lovely girl in the first flush of beauty. The goddess whispered in her dreams, putting it in her mind that soon she would be married, and that she should take a wagon down to the washing-place near the sea to launder all her fine clothes in preparation for the ceremony.

So next day Nausicaa and her maids went down to the washing-place. They took a basket full of fine foods and wine, and a flask of soft olive oil to rub into their skin after bathing, for they intended to make a holiday of it.

The girls washed the clothes, and laid them to dry by the sea's edge. Then they bathed, and anointed themselves with the olive oil, and afterwards they played at catch, tossing a ball from one to the other to the rhythm of Nausicaa's singing.

At last one of the girls threw too hard. The ball went into the sea with a splash, and they all shrieked.

That was Athene's signal. She caused Odysseus to wake. He staggered out from behind the bush that had hidden him, with only a bough wrenched from the undergrowth to cover his nakedness. To the girls he seemed like some wild creature, and they fled from him. Only Nausicaa stood her ground, for Athene had filled her heart with courage.

Odysseus said, "Fair lady, if you are a lady and not a goddess, have pity on me. Tell me, what land is this where I have been cast ashore?"

"This is the country of the Phaeacians, and I am Nausicaa, daughter of its king, Alcinous. You are welcome, stranger, for though you look rough, your words are gentle. Bathe, dress, and come with me to my father's palace, and he will give you all that is due to a guest, for Zeus himself is the patron of the wayfaring stranger."

Alcinous welcomed the castaway with great kindness. He could see that this was no ordinary man; indeed, Athene cast such a glow about Odysseus that he seemed like one of the immortals.

"Tell me what I can do for you," said the king.

"Give me a ship to take me home," answered Odysseus.

"It shall be done," said Alcinous. "But first, you must recover from your ordeal. Go and rest now, and tomorrow I will prepare a ship to take you wherever you wish; and in your honour I will hold a great banquet, and games in which our young men can show you what we Phaeacians are made of."

Next day, Odysseus, who had still not told Alcinous his name, sat in the place of honour at the feast. When everyone had eaten and drunk their fill, Demodocus the blind bard took down his lyre. The goddess inspired him to sing of heroes, and the story he chose told of the quarrel between Odysseus and Achilles, outside the walls of Troy. Odysseus drew his cloak over his face, so that no one should see the tears that ran down his cheeks.

Then Alcinous announced the start of the games. The young Phaeacians vied with one another at running, wrestling, jumping, and throwing the discus, each hoping to impress the noble stranger with their strength and skill.

The best of them all was named Euryalus, and this young man approached Odysseus, saying, "Now it is your turn to show us what you are made of. For no one can be called a man unless he excels at some sport or another."

"I have no taste for such things today," said Odysseus. "My heart is aching to be home."

Euryalus sneered, "You speak like some penny-pinching merchant, whose only pleasure is to count the goods in and out of his warehouse, not like a man of spirit."

Odysseus said, "The gods do not give all their blessings to one man. You have the body of a young hero, but an empty head. Once I too was young and strong, but I have suffered much through the malice of the gods. Yet even now I will accept your challenge at any sport, even running, though I have been sorely battered by the waves."

So Euryalus picked up a discus and threw it as far as he could. "Beat that," he said.

Odysseus rose and took a discus. As he swung back his cloak, the crowd gasped at the corded muscles of his upper arm. He threw, and the discus sailed powerfully through the air, far outstripping Euryalus's throw.

"I am afraid my strength is not what it was," said Odysseus, and everyone laughed, except Euryalus.

Then King Alcinous called for dancing, and the moment was forgotten.

When the dancing was over, Odysseus asked if the bard Demodocus would sing again, and Demodocus sang the deeds of Odysseus and Menelaus at the sack of Troy.

Once more, glittering tears welled from Odysseus's eyes. When the story had come to its end, he said, "Alcinous, you have done me every honour and given me many gifts, and have not so much as asked my name.

"So now I will tell you. I am Odysseus, son of Laertes, Prince of Ithaca. Since the fall of Troy, I have been wandering the seas, buffeted by fate and the gods from one horror to the next. But now, with your help, I hope to reach my home at last."

"Your ship is ready," replied Alcinous, "and you need have no fear of shipwreck. We Phaeacians use no steering-oars, for our ships respond to our very thoughts and skim across the waves with ease and grace. Your long journey is coming to its end."

The Return to Ithaca

The Phaeacian ship carried Odysseus swiftly and safely to Ithaca. When it arrived, Odysseus himself was in a sound slumber, sent by the goddess Athene, and the sailors could not wake him. So they carried him ashore, still wrapped in his blanket, and laid him gently down, together with the rich gifts that he had received from King Alcinous.

But the generous spirit of the Phaeacians did not please Poseidon. As a lesson to King Alcinous, Poseidon waited until the ship had reached the Phaeacian harbour on its homeward journey, and then turned it into solid stone, so that it sank to the sea bottom with all its crew. No man can defy the gods.

Meanwhile Odysseus was stirring from his spellbound sleep. All around him was thick mist. "Where am I?" he groaned. "Have these Phaeacians betrayed me?"

Athene with her gleaming eyes stepped out of the murk, in the guise of a simple shepherd. "You ask where this is," she said. "It is an isle whose fame has travelled far. You are in Ithaca."

Odysseus could have shouted for joy, but instead he said cautiously, "I have heard of the place."

Then Athene took her own shape, a woman, tall and stately, with a beauty that shone from within. She laughed. "You think to hide your identity. But clever as you are, you cannot deceive me. For you are speaking to a god. You cannot hide anything from me."

"If this is Ithaca," said Odysseus, "then I beg you, show it to me." So Athene dispelled the mist, and Odysseus fell to his knees to kiss the soil of his homeland.

Then Athene told him of Penelope's plight, beset by so many bullying suitors. "I will go to Sparta to fetch your son Telemachus home. At the court of King Menelaus he has earned men's respect, and he has matured into a fine man. Meanwhile, you must go to the hut of the old swineherd, Eumaeus. He has remained loyal to Penelope and Telemachus, and will help us in our plans. But first I will make sure that no one here will recognize you."

With that, Athene touched Odysseus with her wand. His hair turned grey, his skin became wrinkled and old, his eyes lost their brightness, and his body bent. His clothes turned into filthy old rags. The goddess gave him a staff and a beggar's bag, and he looked every inch an aged vagabond.

In this guise, Odysseus made his way to Eumaeus's hut. The swineherd's dogs leaped out at him, barking and slavering, and nearly knocked him to the ground, but they stopped at Eumaeus's command. "Welcome, stranger," the swineherd said. "If I can offer you any food or service, I will be happy to, in the hope that some other man will do the same for my noble master, Odysseus, should he by chance be travelling poor and friendless through some strange land. Oh, that he would come home!"

"My friend," said Odysseus, "may the gods reward your kindness, and grant you your desire."

And the pair settled down around the swineherd's fire, to eat and talk and sleep, as old men do.

The goddess Athene left Odysseus sleeping in the swineherd's hut, and went swiftly to Sparta, to the bedside of Telemachus.

She found him tossing and turning, tormented by worry for his father and mother.

Her eyes flashed with sympathy. She told him, "It is time to take your leave of King Menelaus, and return to Ithaca. Do not waste a moment. And when you reach the shore, go straight to the hut of the swineherd Eumaeus."

Telemachus roused himself. By dawn, horses were already harnessed to his chariot; he stayed only long enough to say farewell to his host, before setting out for his ship.

He stood at the prow, urging the ship across the waves, longing to be home.

Meanwhile Odysseus spent the day with Eumaeus, questioning him closely about events on the island. Eumaeus told him everything, never dreaming that the old beggar to whom he spoke was Odysseus himself.

Odysseus already knew of his mother's death, for he had spoken to her shade in the land of the dead. But now he heard firsthand from the loyal swineherd about the loutish behaviour of the suitors, and Telemachus's journey in quest of his father.

That night, Odysseus slept once more in the swineherd's hut. And as dawn lit up the sky, he was woken by the sound of the dogs whimpering. They were not barking, as they would at a stranger, but greeting some long-lost friend.

It was a tall young man, fit and strong. He carried a spear tipped with bronze.

"It is some fine young warrior," said Odysseus.

Eumaeus, wiping the sleep from his bleary eyes, replied, "It is Telemachus, come home at last!" And he embraced his young master, weeping for joy.

So it was that Odysseus laid eyes for the first time on the grown son whom he had left as a baby.

Telemachus felt the old wanderer's eyes on him, and met his glance. "Welcome, stranger," he said. "Though it is a poor welcome I can offer, who dare not even go to my own home for fear of the treachery and murder I read in the suitors' eyes." Then he turned to Eumaeus. "Old friend, please go and tell my mother that I am home, and find out how the land lies before I return to my father's palace."

As soon as Eumaeus had gone, the goddess Athene approached the hut. Only Odysseus could see her, for the immortals are only visible to mortals when they so choose. But the dogs must have sensed her, for they slunk away, whining and trembling with fear.

Athene beckoned Odysseus to come outside. There she told him, "The time has come to act." She touched him with her wand, and he changed back to his own appearance – if anything, stronger and younger and more handsome than before.

When he returned to the hut, Telemachus, already unsettled by the dogs, started back in terror. "Are you a god?" he asked.

"I am no god," said Odysseus. "I am Odysseus, Prince of Ithaca, returned to claim what is mine. It was the goddess Athene who disguised me as an old man. For just as the gods themselves seem now old, now young, now man, now woman, so they have the power to transform us mortals as they choose."

With that, father and son fell into each other's arms, weeping with joy. After Odysseus's long journey, and Telemachus's long search, they had found each other at last. Now, they could face the suitors together.

"Together," said Odysseus, "we shall scour the palace clean of those vermin."

"But how can that be?" asked Telemachus. "There are only two of us, and over a hundred of them, all spoiling for a fight."

"With Athene and Zeus on our side, we do not need any further allies,"

replied Odysseus. "Telemachus, you must go to the palace. I will follow, once more disguised as an old man. The suitors will mock me, and even threaten me. Do not let your anger show. The time will soon come when they bitterly regret every cruel word or unkind blow.

"When the goddess sends me a sign, I will nod to you. Then you must take down every weapon and piece of armour in the hall, and hide them away upstairs. Tell the suitors that you do not want the weapons tarnished by the smoke from the fire, and also that you wish to prevent any quarrel among them from getting out of hand.

"Leave just two swords, two spears, and two shields. Those are for us."

A Beggar at the Door

When Telemachus arrived at the palace, he was greeted by his old nurse Eurycleia, and by his mother Penelope. Both were in tears at his return.

Then the suitors thronged around him, bidding him welcome with their lips but looking murder from their eyes.

Things might have turned ugly, had not Medon, one of the few faithful servants, called the men to the table, to celebrate Telemachus's return. None of the suitors had any qualms about enjoying yet another feast at Odysseus's expense.

As they were dining, Odysseus came to the palace, disguised as an old beggar. Outside the doors to the courtyard, he saw an old dog lying neglected on a dungheap; it was Argus, his faithful hound, who had been waiting patiently all through the long years for his master's return. No disguise could have prevented Argus from knowing Odysseus. The old dog, too crippled and starved to move, wagged his mangy tail. He had lived on beyond his time, hoping against hope for his master's return. Now Argus' faithfulness was repaid, and he died content.

So it was that when Odysseus stumbled across the threshold of his palace, like a failing old man, dressed in rags and leaning on a stick, his head was swimming with sadness. He had to sit down and rest against a pillar.

Athene appeared to him, saying, "Go to each of the suitors in turn, and beg from them. That way you may test if any are worthy to be spared."

Odysseus wandered from man to man, with outstretched hands and whining voice, begging for alms.

Some of the men grudgingly gave him a crust of bread, but none spared him a kind word. Antinous was one of the meanest and most cruel of them. "Go away, old man" he said, "Don't slobber over the table; you're putting me off my meal."

"A fine man like you should have pity on a wretch like me," replied Odysseus. "Once I was rich, and then I never turned a beggar from my door."

"Then it's your own fault you're poor now," retorted Antinous, and all the suitors laughed.

Odysseus felt his anger rising. "You begrudge me a pinch of salt or a crust of bread, yet you sit there gorging on another's meat." And he turned and walked away.

Antinous, outraged at being spoken to in such tones by a mere beggar, lashed out with a stool, catching Odysseus a terrible blow on the back, below his right shoulder. But Odysseus did not stagger. He took the force of the blow and walked on, shaking his head.

At that moment another beggar came into the hall. This was a man named Irus, who though young and strong had never worked, preferring to live by begging. Seeing Odysseus, he cried, "Get out, old man, or I will throw you out. There is no place for you here."

"I have no quarrel with you," said Odysseus. "These men have enough to spare for both of us, for no man dare refuse a beggar, knowing that the gods who have given him health and riches can also take them away."

But Antinous, eager to see the insolent beggar beaten and driven away, shouted, "Let the two beggars make a match of it. The winner shall eat his fill!"

The suitors rose from the table and made a circle round Irus and Odysseus. Their jeers and mockery died in their mouths when Odysseus hitched up his rags and they saw his strong thighs. "This old man is not as feeble as he looks," they muttered.

Irus, who had thought to win an easy victory, began to shake with fear. He lashed out, striking Odysseus on the shoulder. Then Odysseus swung his mighty arm, and crunched his fist into Irus's neck. He fell heavily to the floor, blood pouring from his mouth.

Odysseus took hold of Irus by the leg and dragged him from the room. "You can sit out here among the dogs and swine," he said, dumping Irus in the courtyard. Odysseus returned to join the feast.

The suitors made merry till nightfall, and Odysseus tended the fire. But at last they retired to their beds, and then Odysseus nodded to Telemachus, "It is time to take down the weapons from the wall." And while Telemachus saw to this, Odysseus waited by the fire.

Now Penelope came into the hall, to see if this beggar had any news of Odysseus. He comforted her with words, telling her that he had heard Odysseus was even then returning to his home.

Penelope called her serving maids, and told them to wash the beggar's hands and feet, to find him a place to rest, and treat him as an honoured guest, for he had spoken of her husband with such gentleness.

Now the serving maids were lazy creatures, more often to be found in some dark corner with one of the suitors than by Penelope's side, and they shrank from the old beggar. But Eurycleia, the old nurse, who had cared for Odysseus when he was a baby, willingly fetched a bronze basin, and filled it with water to bathe the beggar's weary feet.

While she was bathing his leg, she felt an old scar above his knee, where Odysseus had been gored by a wild boar, and she knew her master at once. But he put his finger to her lips. "Do not betray me." So Eurycleia did not say a word, though her heart was filled with a trembling joy.

"Stranger," said Penelope. "I have one more question. I dreamed last night that a great eagle came down from the mountains and slaughtered all my white geese. What can it mean?"

"Surely," replied Odysseus, "your dream meant that the eagle was Odysseus, come to take his vengeance on the suitors."

"Dreams are of two kinds," said Penelope. "Some come to us through the gate of ivory, and these dreams are false. But others, Morpheus, the god of sleep, sends to us through the gate of horn, and these are true visions.

"I wish your interpretation were true," she went on. "For now the suitors have discovered the trick by which I have kept them at bay, and my tapestry is finished. Tomorrow, I must choose between them. As a test, I will set up twelve axes in a line. Odysseus used to do this, and shoot an arrow through the rings in their handles, a feat no other man could match. If anyone tomorrow can manage it, I will be his bride."

That night, Penelope lay weeping on her bed, dreading the morning. But at last Athene granted her the blessing of sleep.

Odysseus lay down on a fleece by the dying embers of the fire. As he thought of the suitors, his heart growled for vengeance like a wild beast ravening its prey.

Odysseus's Revenge

The next day was a feast day in honour of Apollo, the god of archery, who fires the golden arrows of the sun.

Penelope went to the storeroom where Odysseus had left his most precious treasures, and fetched down his carved and crafted bow, and its quiver full of deadly arrows.

She asked Telemachus to bury the twelve axes headfirst in the ground, with their ringed handles sticking up.

Medon the steward summoned the suitors, and Telemachus explained to them that whoever could string Odysseus's bow, and shoot an arrow through all twelve axes, would win his mother's hand.

Antinous laughed. "This is too easy," he said. "Even Leodes here," and Antinous pointed at the weakest of them all, "could do it."

Everyone jeered as Leodes picked up the bow. But he could not bend it to fit the string, nor could any of the others, though they strained with all their might. Finally Antinous himself tried, but he was no more successful.

Then Odysseus rose, "Let me try." he said, "I once was a fine bowman. Let me see if I still have any strength left."

"Are you mad?" asked Antinous. "Do you think you, a nameless wanderer, could succeed where we princes have failed? You must be drunk."

Odysseus took the bow. He caressed it, feeling carefully for any weakness, but the bow was as sound as ever. He took the string, and attached it with as little effort as a master musician replacing the string on his lyre. It twanged beneath his fingers with a low, pure, menacing tone that drained the colour from the suitors' cheeks, even as they watched him.

Then Zeus let his thunder rumble across the sky, and Odysseus laughed

at this sign of the great god's favour. He took an arrow and fired it, straight and true, through the axes. He took a second, and loosed the bow again. Antinous fell gurgling on to the table, with an arrow through his neck.

At first the suitors thought the old beggar had fired in error, but then they saw Telemachus step to his side, sword and spear in hand. Odysseus's voice boomed through the hall. "You curs. You thought that Odysseus would never return. You made yourselves at home in his palace, eating his food, drinking his drink, wooing his wife and corrupting his servants. But I am back, and you are doomed."

With that, Odysseus and Telemachus, aided by the goddess Athene, who watched in the shape of a swallow perched on the roof-beam, set on the suitors, and slaughtered every one. The last was cowardly Leodes, who threw his arms around Odysseus's legs to beg for mercy, but Odysseus

severed his head before the words had left his mouth.

However, Odysseus spared the bard Phemius, who had sung for the suitors, for he would not kill one who was inspired by the gods.

And in the silence after the battle, the faithful steward Medon crawled out unhurt from beneath a chair, where he had hidden from Odysseus's whirlwind of vengeance.

All about them, the bodies of the suitors lay heaped, like the silver harvest that fishermen pour out of their nets on to the white sand.

Odysseus ordered Medon to see that the corpses were removed, the room cleaned, and a new fire kindled. Then he unlocked the door to the women's quarters, and called for Eurycleia. When the old nurse saw the suitors lying dead she could have shouted for joy, but Odysseus told her, "It is wrong to rejoice over any man's death, even your enemy. It is the will of the gods whether we live or die. Now, go and tell your mistress that I have returned, and what has happened here."

But Penelope, who had been sitting with her maids listening to the bloodcurdling cries from the hall, would not believe that her saviour was Odysseus. "It must be some god who has done this thing," she said. "And besides, I could not fail to know my own husband, whatever suffering he had endured. Odysseus is dead."

"No," said Eurycleia. "This is Odysseus. When I washed his feet, I saw the scar on his leg."

So Penelope went down to the hall.

Odysseus was sitting against a pillar on one side of the great fire. Penelope did not go to embrace him, but instead sat on the other side of the fire. She remained there in silence, gazing at the old beggarman in his filthy rags. Sometimes as the firelight flickered across his face he did have a look of Odysseus; sometimes he seemed a complete stranger.

"You must be tired," she said to him. She turned to Eurycleia. "Have the maids fetch the bed from our bridal chamber, and make it up."

"What do you mean?" Odysseus said angrily. "It's not possible to move

my bed, I built it myself around an olive tree, and used the tree's trunk for the bedpost. Unless someone has cut through the trunk, the bed cannot be taken out of the room."

And then Penelope knew that this was indeed Odysseus, and she ran into his arms.

Outside, the night air echoed with the twittering of the suitors' souls as they journeyed down to Hades.

Wise Athene gave back Odysseus his own appearance, and Penelope's happiness was complete.

Penelope and Odysseus embraced in the fire's glow, their troubles at an end. Now Odysseus's long wanderings were over, and he was at peace with the gods at last.

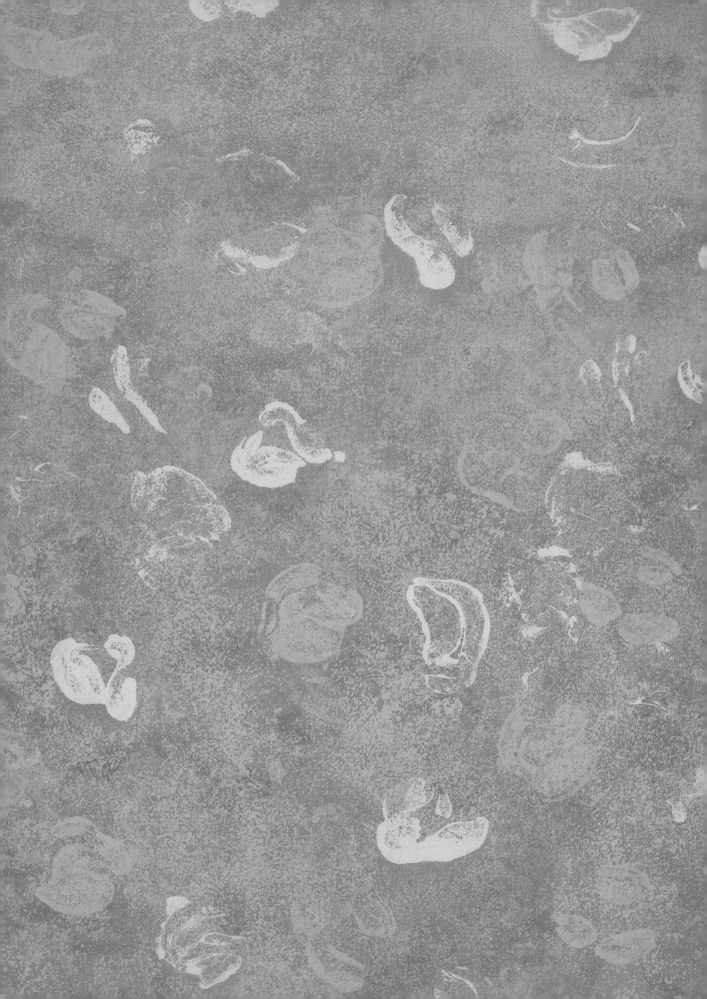